2/11

PET CARE LIBRARY

Caring for Your Hamster

by Derek Zobel

THREE RIVERS PUBLIC LIBRARY
25207 W. CHANNON DRIVE
P.O. BOX 300
CHANNAHON, IL 60410-0300

BLASTOFF!
4
READERS

BELLWETHER MEDIA • MINNEAPOLIS, MN

Note to Librarians, Teachers, and Parents:

Blastoff! Readers are carefully developed by literacy experts and combine standards-based content with developmentally appropriate text.

Level 1 provides the most support through repetition of high-frequency words, light text, predictable sentence patterns, and strong visual support.

Level 2 offers early readers a bit more challenge through varied simple sentences, increased text load, and less repetition of high-frequency words.

Level 3 advances early-fluent readers toward fluency through increased text and concept load, less reliance on visuals, longer sentences, and more literary language.

Level 4 builds reading stamina by providing more text per page, increased use of punctuation, greater variation in sentence patterns, and increasingly challenging vocabulary.

Level 5 encourages children to move from "learning to read" to "reading to learn" by providing even more text, varied writing styles, and less familiar topics.

Whichever book is right for your reader, Blastoff! Readers are the perfect books to build confidence and encourage a love of reading that will last a lifetime!

This edition first published in 2011 by Bellwether Media, Inc.

No part of this publication may be reproduced in whole or in part without written permission of the publisher. For information regarding permission, write to Bellwether Media, Inc., Attention: Permissions Department, 5357 Penn Avenue South, Minneapolis, MN 55419.

Library of Congress Cataloging-in-Publication Data

Zobel, Derek, 1983-
Caring for your hamster / by Derek Zobel.
   p. cm. – (Pet care library) (Blastoff! readers)
Includes bibliographical references and index.
Summary: "Developed by literacy experts for students in grades two through five, this title provides readers with basic information for taking care of hamsters"–Provided by publisher.
ISBN 978-1-60014-468-4 (hardcover : alk. paper)
1. Hamsters as pets–Juvenile literature. I. Title.
SF459.H3Z63 2011
636.935'6–dc22   2010017681

Text copyright © 2011 by Bellwether Media, Inc. BLASTOFF! READERS and associated logos are trademarks and/or registered trademarks of Bellwether Media, Inc.

Printed in the United States of America, North Mankato, MN.
080110   1162

Contents

Choosing a Hamster

Hamsters are small, cute animals that make good pets. They bond well with their owners.

Although a hamster lives in a cage, it is still a big responsibility. You will need to play with and feed your hamster every day. Most hamsters live about 2 to 5 years.

Care Tip

Some hamsters live best in pairs. If you get more than one hamster, do not choose a male and a female. If you do, you might end up with a lot of baby hamsters!

Russian

Roborovski

Syrian

There are many hamster **breeds**. Each breed has different **traits** and behaviors. Some are social, while others like to live alone. Be sure to choose a hamster that is right for you.

Supply List

Here is a list of supplies you will
need to take care of a hamster.

- hamster cage
- food dish
- hamster food
- water bottle
  with drip feed
- bedding
- chewing blocks
- hamster wheel
- hamster ball
- nesting box

You can get your hamster from a pet store
or a **breeder**. Wherever you get your
hamster, you will need supplies from a pet
store to properly take care of it.

Setting Up a Hamster Cage

Care Tip

If you choose a metal cage, your hamster will have something to climb on. Just make sure your hamster can't fit between the bars!

Bring your hamster home in a small box filled with **bedding**. Your hamster will need a large cage to live in. You can use a metal cage or a plastic cage. Metal cages are easier to clean and let in fresh air for your hamster.

Add fun things to your hamster's cage. Plastic tunnels are a good choice. Hamsters enjoy crawling through and exploring tunnels.

Care Tip

Your hamster's cage needs to be cleaned weekly. Scoop out old bedding and wash the cage with warm, soapy water. Then fill the cage with new bedding.

Cover the bottom of the cage with bedding. Add a **nesting box** to give your hamster a nice place to sleep.

Put your hamster's cage in a cool, quiet place away from direct sunlight. Hamsters sleep a lot during the day. They are **nocturnal**.

nesting box

bedding

Feeding Your Hamster

Your hamster will need a food dish. It should be heavy, **ceramic**, and have straight sides so it cannot tip over. Make sure to always keep it full of dry hamster food.

For variety, your hamster should also eat fruits and vegetables a few times a week. A small piece of apple, pear, strawberry, carrot, or broccoli makes a nice treat.

Your hamster's cage should have a water bottle. A special water bottle with a steel **drip feed** is best. Refill the bottle with fresh water every day.

water bottle ➡

drip feed

If your hamster stops eating or drinking, take it to a **veterinarian**. It might be sick and need special care or medicine.

Exercise and Play

hamster
wheel

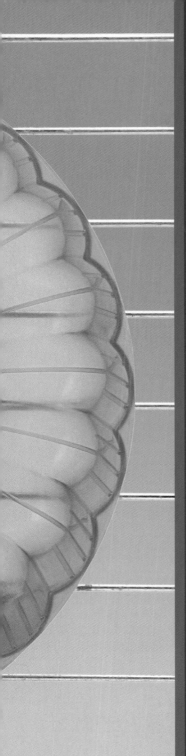

To stay happy and healthy, your hamster will need to exercise and explore. Add some toys to the cage for your hamster to play with and chew.

Your hamster can run in a **hamster wheel** to get exercise. The wheel should be solid, plastic, and attached to the side of the cage. A metal hamster wheel can be dangerous.

Ramps and empty toilet paper rolls are also good toys for hamsters. Put a few in the cage and move them around every week. This gives your hamster new places to explore.

hamster ball

Care Tip

Hamsters enjoy chewing blocks made of wood. The blocks can help keep your hamster's teeth healthy.

Outside of the cage, hamsters can play in a **hamster ball**. Be sure the lid is secure, and keep your hamster away from steps. Never leave your hamster alone in its ball.

You and Your Hamster

You should hold your hamster at least once a day. It needs to get used to your voice and smell. Play with it close to the ground so it will not get hurt if it falls.

To know how your hamster is feeling, look at its ears. If they are folded back, your hamster is tired. If they are perky, your hamster is ready to play!

! fun fact

When your hamster gets scared, it might puff out its cheeks or even play dead!

Glossary

bedding—material that hamsters use to make nests; bedding should cover the bottom of a hamster's cage.

breeder—a person who raises hamsters and sells them to other people

breeds—types of hamsters

ceramic—made of clay

drip feed—a tube-shaped part at the end of a hamster's water bottle; a drip feed has a ball inside that a hamster has to push in order to drink water.

hamster ball—a hollow ball that a hamster can play in; a hamster runs inside a hamster ball to make it roll and move forward.

hamster wheel—a wheel that a hamster can run in to get exercise; hamster wheels should be solid, plastic, and attached to the side of the cage.

nesting box—a box where a hamster makes a nest and sleeps

nocturnal—awake and active at night; nocturnal animals sleep during the day.

traits—qualities

veterinarian—a doctor who takes care of animals

To Learn More

AT THE LIBRARY

Foran, Jill. *Caring for Your Hamster*. Mankato, Minn.: Weigl Publishers, 2003.

Landau, Elaine. *Your Pet Hamster*. New York, N.Y.: Children's Press, 2007.

Sabatés, Berta García, and Mercé Segarra. *Let's Take Care of Our New Hamster*. Hauppauge, N.Y.: Barron's Educational, 2008.

ON THE WEB

Learning more about pet care is as easy as 1, 2, 3.

1. Go to www.factsurfer.com.

2. Enter "pet care" into the search box.

3. Click the "Surf" button and you will see a list of related Web sites.

With factsurfer.com, finding more information is just a click away.

Index

The images in this book are reproduced through the courtesy of: Eric Isselée, front cover; Janet Bailey/Masterfile, front cover (small); Michael Krabs/Photolibrary, pp. 4-5; Alex Kalashnikov, p. 6 (top); His Light Productions, p. 6 (middle); Klara Salamo ska, p. 6 (bottom); Juniors Bildarchiv/Age Fotostock, pp. 6-7; Juniors Bildarchiv/Photolibrary, pp. 8-9, 12-13, 13 (small), 14, 15, 16-17, 20-21; Juan Martinez, p. 9 (small); Klein-Hubert/KimballStock, pp. 10-11; imagebroker/Alamy, p. 18; John Howard/Getty Images, p. 19; C. Steimer/Age Fotostock, p. 19 (small).